Musings Of The 21st Century

Adya Niraj

BookLeaf Publishing

India | USA | UK

Dedication

To my family

(A term I do not use loosely, so you know who you are!)

Preface

My mother calls me a deep thinker (not an overthinker, mind you). She believes that some of my thoughts are quite interesting and should be written down in a book—or at least a blog. I finally gave in, and this collection of poems is a bunch of thoughts from a young person navigating the challenges and amusing aspects of life as we know it today.

These poems don't follow any particular pattern. One moment, you might be moved by something motivational; the next, you'll find a ridiculous—and hopefully humorous—take on how hard it is to keep my plants alive.

As a poet, I do hope my poems appeal to your literary senses and bring a smile to your face—or even a tear to your eye. But more than anything, I wish for you, the reader, to relate to this book. We all have good days, bad days, days when we feel anxious, days when we're totally unimpressed by the world, and days when we feel on top of it. I believe that's what being human is all about. In this book, you'll get a sense of the kind of day I was having when I wrote each poem.

So yes, I've included a variety of emotions throughout this book, but I hope that by the end, you're left with a lasting feeling of hope—that after every night comes the sun, and that on days when it's hard to keep your spirits high, it helps to move through life with a touch of humor and absurdity.

Acknowledgements

Very few people reach their goals entirely on their own. No matter how self-reliant one may consider themselves, it is the little things—and the big things—done by those around them that make it possible to achieve a dream.

I've always written poems, and it's been my dream since childhood to write books. But it takes an army to turn dreams into reality. This idle dream of mine has been fueled over the years by the people closest to me who pushed me to do something about it.

My mother, Dr Smita Gupta, plays the biggest role here. She has never ridiculed a single dream of mine for as long as I can remember. I studied law, became a classical dancer, participated in Miss India, completed an MBA from the best institute in India, and now, I've written my first book—all because of this woman who refuses to believe there is anything I cannot achieve. As with every other pursuit of mine, she has been by my side, reviewing and editing my poems. Every time I wrote one, I'd send it to her and wait nervously for her honest, critical feedback.

The love of my life and my best friend, Kshitij, has taken my life on a whirlwind journey since I met him five years ago. His high energy and go-getter attitude have constantly pushed me to never settle—for less, or for anything below what I truly deserve. On the days I felt dejected or too lazy to continue with this project, Kshitij wouldn't let it slide. He made sure I got up, got to work, and followed through on the commitment I had made to myself.

I would also like to acknowledge my siblings, Vinayak and Satakshi. Because of the age gap between us, I often consider them more like my children and view their successes with tearful, proud eyes. One of the biggest things I've learned from them is persistence. Unlike me, when they start a project or hobby, they rarely abandon it halfway. I'm blessed to be surrounded by such motivated people—they truly inspire me.

Lastly, I want to thank my future readers. The thought of you picking up this book and giving me your time has kept me going. This is all for you, and hopefully, it's just the beginning of our long journey together.

1. The 21st Century Woman

"Hell hath no fury like a woman scorned",
Especially when her choices are torn
In the 21st century, women rise,
of all shapes, sizes, and colors, with diverse guise

From doctors to artists, to homemakers too,
They're born into or choose to embrace their
womanhood anew,
Dare to scorn her, her hustle, or her name,
And you'll face the fury of a modern woman's flame

She doesn't back down, she fights with might,
She loses, wins, and rises again with sprite
Her standards are high, her spirit won't break,
She'll never stop fighting for what she believes she'll
make

She'll take on the society, the ideologies, and social
media's goons,
And anyone who says she's not enough, she will chase
them to the moon.
Because hell hath no fury like a 21st-century woman
scorned,
With a fire that burns, and a spirit that's reborn.

2. The 21st Century Man

The 21st Century man,
Demure and firm,
Masculine and feminine,
Embracing that the essence of being a male,

Not restricted to a few monotonous boxes,
To be a male in the 21st century is to be free,
Free of the notions of masculinity,
Free of demands to aggress

Yet the world tries to regress
And contain the newfound male freedom,
But damn, once the freedom is tasted
It won't go wasted

Once the dams of emotional suppression are open,
There is no going back,
With a few hiccups in between,
The male will learn to cut himself some slack

Ying and yang are not so non-porous,
Opposite genders interchange their roles,
The 21st century man happily knows,
This fluidity, this freedom to grow.

3. Go Big or Go Home

Sometimes I wonder,
At the source of the thunder,
All of us expected to carry,
Crack inhuman exams, get loaded with a job, and marry?

Who is setting these expectations?
The need for society's felicitations?
Are they coming from within,
Or, are families driving the chagrin?

Because if all of us are to be the best,
The math doesn't add to the rest.
Some will naturally be left behind,
Lost in the turmoil to grind!

But is being left behind so bad?
Maybe hustling is just a fad.
A 21st century mindset,
Which needs to bc reset.

Our grandparents led a calm life,
Their lives were not laced with strife,
With the need to reach the top,
Else you will be called a flop!

How can being a human be so monotonous,
Bent on a book and laptop continuous?
We need to step out and feel,
Layers of life and nature, we must peel.

Because a human is not a robot.
Confined within four walls, will rot.
Our flesh and blood bodies,
Reject your dull success stories!

Let's break free from this suffocating mold,
And find our own path, our own gold.
Let's live life on our own terms,
And find joy in the simple, quiet concerns.

4. Seeking Help

Weakness is not wrong,
We mustn't always be strong,
The 21st Century ensures to teach us this,
You don't need to act like your life is a constant bliss.

The pressures of our times,
Can get to the most resilient minds.
But unlike not a few years before,
Nobody is embarrassed of the troubled mind's lore.

Mental hiccups recently came my way,
Couldn't keep anxiety at bay,
Thought the world was closing up on me,
From the shackles of fear, how do I get free?

The bottomless ocean of depression,
Brooding becoming an obsession,
But hell, I wasn't alone in it,
My family and friends ensured to do their bit.

Their calming reassurances and patient ear,
Made me realize that there is nothing to fear,
My mind may start acting an enemy,
But surrounded I am, with priceless bonhomie.

Pathway to recovery came into sight,
My support systems aligned with me to fight,
And they did set my mind right,
Once again joyful and light!

Seeking help is the best,
Sets your troubled mind to rest,
And in case you do not have friends and family abound,
We are fortunate to be alive in times when other
resources surround.

Tap into them and pour your heart out,
The darkness in your mind will lose its clout,
Because blessed are we to live in this time,
When the world is screaming to us, you'll be fine!

5. Mother

To the brave woman,
Who said I could achieve anything,
Her doting eyes, my forever zing.

To the brave woman,
Who said no setback can define my life,
Everything would always turn out fine.

To the brave woman,
Who is a force of positivity,
Luckiest I am, she supports my creativity.

To the brave woman,
Who is also my best pal,
The wisest and silliest, she's my go-to gal!

To the brave woman,
Who is unafraid to love,
I look at you in awe, my personal angel from heaven
above.

To the brave woman,
You make me so proud,
With time, to newer qualities of yours I have bowed.

To the brave woman,

My gratefulness is profound,

For ensuring that in your daughter, braveness is abound!

6. Furry Children

The 21st century human,
Procreate they may,
But not always a babe of their species,
Sometimes those with bodies covered in fur!

From companions to children,
These furry beings have climbed the ladder,
They no longer survive on morsels of kindness,
But rule the household as a whiny child may.

The 21st century human,
Dotes and spoils their furry children,
In return for unbridled affection,
Which otherwise might be scarce to find.

From companions to children,
These furry beings are aware of the power they hold,
The power is not limited to the ones in stores with shiny
mane,
But has seeped into the bones of even the stray!

The 21st century human,
Brings these purry and drooly beings home to the
disdain of many!

But even the patriarchs and matriarchs get defeated,
By the power of adorableness that the furry beings
exercise.

From companions to children,
Ambition of world domination by the furry beings is
real,
Humankind has already lost the war,
We are puppets dancing to their tune, oh dear!

7. Clueless Heart

What is it that the heart desires?
Amidst laughter it hides tears.
A gloom that unfurls in times unpredictable,
Rendering guileless moments despicable.
Tiresome to understand,
The predicament of the heart, too fuddled to stand,
Anointed in the mess, is the mind,
Annoyingly mature, it shuts the heart's desire to find.

8. Sunflower in My Soul

Do not mistake me for a bloom of spring,
A broad smile, and a sunny bling,
For I am not always poetry
Which can light your face.
Instead of warming your heart,
I might put it on fire,
And you will burn along my pyre!
Because I may bring spring,
But, also rain and gloom,
My soul is full of sunflowers,
Yet, the heart bleeds with thorny roses.
Nights of merry making are not so common,
As those spent in dingy hospital corridors,
Awaiting for the sun to rise again.

Been through so much,
Yet, I keep coming back!
Because the sun rises without fail,
And the sunflower in my soul turns towards it, as
always,
Even though the night will fall again.

9. Bravehearts

13

Here is to the brave hearts,
The ones who face shattered realities,
Broken dreams, and desperate times,
Yet, they do not lose their spirit and appetite for life.
Who like phoenix rise from ashes,
With a fiercer soul and an unquenchable zest for life!

10. It's My Birthday!

My birthday is here,
No two ways about it, my dear.
There is no mystery surrounding it,
Everyone who values me, must do their bit.

Because I do not belong to the group,
Who act like their birthday is a coup.
Silent and serious; they think birthdays are no big deal.
They don't ask for a fest, just a nice meal.

Well, I strongly disagree,
Birthdays are meant to be full of glee,
Because life is to be celebrated,
And happiness shouldn't be berated.

It is no small feat to just grow old;
Be healthy and happy, amongst the challenges that life unfold.
So yes, I want everyone to sing off-tune,
"Happy birthday to this little girl, who is loved to the moon."

Maybe only by herself,
Because its prime responsibility to love yourself.

And so she will sing and dance,
Because her happiness cannot be left to chance.

So happy birthday to me,
May I forever want my birthdays to be full of glee,
Filled with laughter, love, and delight,
And shine with joy, on this special night.

11. New Kids in Town

Cheerful and dark,
No feelings are met with snark.
The new kids are here,
The ones who hold their values dear.

In times when micro trends rule the season,
Shop till you drop, without reason,
Rampant consumerism leads to waste,
Yet, there is a strong faction which doesn't buy in haste.

Vintage and thrifting is in,
Your old clothes, once held dear, need not go to bin,
Such is the dichotomy of the new gen,
Their kaleidoscopic nature, cannot be described by pen!

But the one colour which pops out,
Is that there is hope, in this generation's snout,
Strong opinions are up to the brim,
These kids are not afraid to address matters grim!

Environment, inclusion or mental health,
The new kids do not believe in stealth,
They loudly address nuanced woes,
Their persistence ensures that community grows.

Things are turning for the better,
Because with these new kids, we leave all matter.
Their rejection of age old norms, we may not understand,
But they do know how to take a stand!

There is hope that they will make the world a better place,
One where everyone will be accepted with grace.
The new kids are in town,
I believe they won't let us down!

12. Desk Job

I am stuck at my desk job,
All my peace, it may rob.
Oh, how I desire to be outside,
Where colours, flowers and actual life reside.

While I'm tapping my fingers on the keyboard,
I think of how I could hit the road,
Explore social media-affirmed magical territories,
And upload my images as my victories.

Oh, the clothes I'll wear on the trip,
And the gluttony; reality will lose its grip!
The beaches that I'll explore,
And the sleepless nights; which won't be a pain
anymore.

Because while I'll be awake, I'll be merry-making,
Not consumed by the dark hues of corporate stress
taking.
And even on Monday morning, I will be fresh as the
dawn,
No more blues will make me yawn.

Because the only blue, will be the endless sea,

Oh, how fun it will be to be finally free.

And with these daydreams, I feel myself smiling.

But eventually, reality strikes, and I am back to whining.

13. Keeping Plants Alive

We strive to keep our plants alive,
But in the end, they do what they want to thrive.

They drop a dead leaf, just to make us fret,
Leaving us to wonder if we're doing it right or incorrect.

Do we water them enough, or is it too much to bear?
Deciding whether a little less or a little more is hard to declare.

Do we keep the soil dry, or is that a mistake?
All these decisions make me anxious, and my heart starts to ache.

I want healthy plants, but despite my care,
They turn gaunt, and I am distraught and scared.

These green goblins call my bluff,
To keep them alive, I huff and puff.

Is it too much to ask for a flower to bloom?
Why do I have no power over these plants that I groom?

I spend a wealth on them, but they seem to yawn.

Yet this one-sided relationship, continues to drag on.

Why can't my plants put an effort to look good?
I coax them with every fertilizing treat, but they seem to
turn to wood.

They act coy, and give my enthusiasm a beat,
Leaving me to wonder if I should just accept defeat.

On the contrary, their wild cousins, unearthed and free,
Grow with gay abandon, and their flowers are a sight to
see.

With no one to take care of them, they thrive.
In stark contrast to my pampered plants, which seem to
struggle to survive.

So what kind of green fingers do I need to manifest?
To stop my plants from making this jest?

I know they have the potential to be healthy as ever,
Yet they never seem to understand my emotions and
endeavor.

14. I am always happy!

Oh yes, I am always happy,
My brain has been wired to reject emotions snappy.

My grinning face is all you see,
On your tiny screens, I am dancing with glee.

You see me eating scrumptious meals,
Wearing the perfect clothes and heels.

My face is plump and shiny with happiness,
The perfect makeup giving my visage wholesomeness.

I'll be seen surrounded by friends,
The boisterous laughter never ends.

But my pictures don't tell how many of them I can call,
On the days when I am feeling small.

My pictures don't tell how many meals I have to skip,
The anxiety of my body turning ugly - a constant grip.

I layer on cosmetics, a daily disguise,
Hoping to hide the flaws which bring tears to my eyes.

My merry-making is just occasional.
To think I am always happy, is delusional!

Because I'm not a robot wired to act and feel optimal,
I'm a human with shades of thoughts and emotions,
subliminal.

So don't get fooled by my pictures on social media,
My grinning face shouldn't give you the wrong idea.

And don't start thinking your life is less,
Because, not so surprisingly, my life is also a mess!

15. The Romantic

To be the girl who dances with abandon,
She smiles and laughs at beauties random.
She appreciates everything for the good in it,
And finds solace even in people misfit.

Such a girl, I'm sorry, only exits in tales;
You can't find her in real females.
The one who is sweetest and will sigh and swoon,
In the real world, may be considered a loon.

Because, while 21st century is pretty inclusive,
People don't entertain thoughts-intrusive.
Oh, such femineity, a divine, ethereal sight,
Untouched beauty, sublime, a wonderous delight!

Well, she can be only found in film,
Because real girls flatulate and belch on whim.
And if you get discomforted by a fact like this,
You should entirely give womankind a miss.

16. Lonely Road

In life's journey, I've often been stuck in a fix,
My mind's been filled with strife, and emotions a mix.

At crossroads, I ponder and weigh,
My options unfold, but peace is far away.

In these moments, I may take the easy route,
Or spice it up and choose a tougher pursuit.

But what if I'm stuck in a rut, feeling blue?
I remind myself that all will be well, it's true.

When worries consume me, and fears take hold,
I recall that greatness is not achieved by growing old.

It's the challenges we face, the trials we bear,
That shape us into stronger, wiser souls, with more to share.

17. Anxiety is My Friend

Anxiety is my friend;
It shows up uninvited, a trend.

I may try to keep it at bay,
But it somehow always creeps into my way.

The more I try to shut it out,
The more it raises its ugly snout.

It wants to embrace me in its smelly arm,
Taking away my peace, to my alarm.

I think the causes of my anxiety are trivial,
Yet somehow it hijacks my mental space, convivial.

Turns it into a place of war,
Obsessing over thoughts that are way too miniature.

Little inconveniences that, if they happened to others,
I would jest, and say they're not trying enough, and
unnecessarily bother.

Yet why does it happen to me so frequently?
My mind starts acting delinquently.

With a few carefree days, I assume it's in the past,
I've defeated anxiety at last.

That I have finally cured my brain with logic,
And ingrained in myself that there's nothing tragic.

Yet anxiety, being my friend, will show up uninvited,
And will again take my peaceful sleep unprompted.

It makes my heart so heavy, I would want to weep.
Oh anxiety, back- off, let me sleep!!

18. Support System

My support systems, or rather survival kit,
The two or three people who know me as a misfit.
I am transparent to them;
They know what makes me overwhelmed.

My anxiety and constant worry,
When life starts looking hazy and blurry,
They know how to clear my view,
So my heart can see the sun anew.

But what do I do when my support systems are away?
They may not be present when my thoughts go astray.
How do I cope with my mind's mess,
When everything starts feeling less?

This is when being an adult strikes me as the worst,
Because as a child, my family would never let my bubble
burst.
Even when the worst nightmares made me weep,
My mother was only a room away to help me sleep.

Now I don't get nightmares anymore,
But I wake up with sleepless thoughts galore.
Who will make me fall back asleep?

I am not in my family's keep.

I am alone, living in a big city,
Trying to make my way through the nitty-gritty.
Who will make me fall back asleep?
The support system within myself, I need to reap.

19. When Life Gives You Lemons

When life gives you lemons,
Make lemonade, lemon tart or lemon pickle.
The crux is to do something about it,
There are so many recipes to be made,
You just have to put in the effort to cook!
When life's numerous troubles unfold,
I'm not preaching; they can be mold,
Into something positive and worthwhile.
But, remember only you are the chef of your life,
You have the capability to cook things anew.
So, when life give you lemons,
Squeeze them, cut them, and change their form.
Make something so delicious,
That the lemons feel that they have been had,
And you'll wonder why did these lemons even make you mad.

20. Self Care

Self-care is a must; we cannot let our bodies rust.
Our roots may teach the best, but they tell us that life is
a test.
Hardship and patience make us win; we must escape the
self-fulfillment spin.

I don't agree with this wish; tending to myself is not
selfish.
I'll care for my physical and spiritual form, breaking
away from the ascetic norm.
I break my back trying to earn bread; I'd better reward
myself for enduring the difficult tread.

All hardworking people, you know who you are –
appreciate yourself to not let your spirit mar.
Whether a corporate girl or a homemaker, you must not
allow your personhood to waver.

Hit the gym, get a manicure, or read a book; don't get
discouraged by scornful looks.
These judgments belong to the past; in the 21st century,
self-care is here to last.

21. Grateful

I'm grateful for everything,
Love, a full tummy, and life with bling.
But no less grateful for the tough days,
The dreams unfulfilled, and failures in many ways.

It may sound preachy,
Coming from someone who leads a life that's beachy ,
But trust me, I haven't attained Zen.
Far from it, I'm extremely terrified of life, even.

In the three decades I've spent on Earth,
I'm proud that hardships don't make me bent.
Contrarily, they remind me that I'm extremely strong,
And my fears couldn't be more wrong.

Failures now provide me with assurance,
That I have strength in huge abundance.
They concretize my resolve,
That for avoiding a challenge, I won't self-absolve.

Because sticks and stones may break my bones,
But they can't snatch my optimistic tones.
I'll try harder to achieve every dream.

So that my future self will reminisce and gratefully beam.

33